LIVING IT UP

CONTEMPORARY SONGS AND SKETCHES FOR YOUTH

by Dennis and Nan Allen

Lillenas PUBLISHING COMPANY
Kansas City, MO 64141

CONTENTS

Living It Up

Words and Music by
SHAWN CRAIG, DAN DEAN
and LEONARD AHLSTROM
Arranged by Dennis Allen

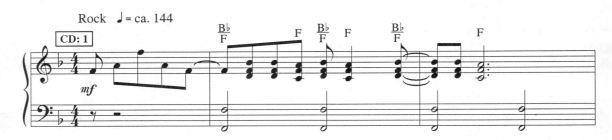

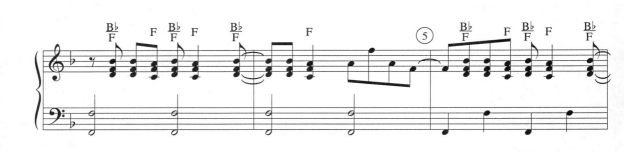

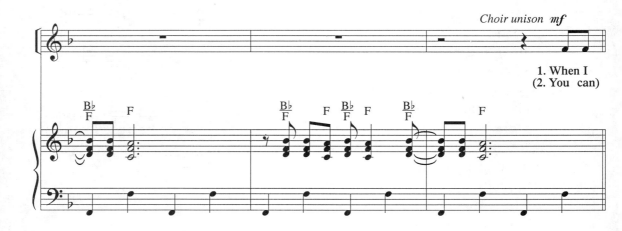

CD: 2 1st time
CD: 4 2nd time

8

STORY HOUR
Sketch

Characters:

#1

#2

#3

Props:

two books

a Bible

a table (large enough for three chairs to sit under it on one side)

(Scene opens as #2 and #3 are sitting at a table, at center, reading as if in a library)

(enter #1 with a book, sits between #2 and #3)

#1:   *(to #2, after a beat or two)* So...what are you reading?

#2:   *(looking somewhat annoyed)* A book. That's what you do at the library.

#1:   Yeah. *(beat)* I'm reading a book, too!

#2:   *(sarcastically)* I'm thrilled for you.

#1:   *(beat)* It's got...a lot of chapters...

#2:   Marvelous. Now if you don't mind...

#1:   Sorry. *(beat)* Ya see, some chapters are action adventure stories. Some are... love stories. *(getting emotional)* They make you cry.

#2:   Excuse me, but I'm trying to read here!!

#3:   Shhhh!

#1:   *(to #2)* Yeah. Shhhh...*(two beats)* And there's science and history and literature.

#2:   Oh, please!!

#3:   Shhhhh!!!!

(#1 points to #2)

#2: *(trying to speak calmly and softer, but very sarcastically)* Listen, why don't you just tell me what you're reading...spill the whole plot...get it all over with...okay?

#1: Well, you don't have to get snippy.

#2: I'm sorry, all right? What's the name of your book?

#1: *(shows #2 the cover)* The Holy Bible.

#2: Fiction, huh?

#1: No. It's all true. It all really happened.

#2: Well...maybe a long time ago.

#1: Yeah. But it's just like it happened yesterday.

#3: *(to #1)* Excuse me. Did you say that book had action...and...history and science?

#1: Sure did. And it's been on the best seller list longer than any other book... ever!

#3: Wow. And I thought my book was good!

#2: Wait a minute, let me see that book.

#1: Sure. *(hands the book to #2)* Here.

#2: *(looking through book)* History, huh? Where?

#1: First page..."In the beginning..."

#3: Whoa! That's definitely ancient history. I love history.

#2: Oh yeah? Well,...what about the science you talked about?

#1: Hey, scientific fact can be found in almost every chapter. The weather, for instance, was the big story in Genesis the seventh chapter. Big flood...one boat...a handful of survivors.

#3: *(to #2)* Let me see that after you!

#2: Not so fast. What about the action adventure stuff?

#1: Action? How 'bout in Exodus 14. The mighty Red Sea parted and a million people walked across on dry land.

#3: Really? I thought that was just in that movie...ya know, with Charlton Heston. *(grabbing for the book)* Let me see.

#2: No, no. *(to #1)* You said there was literature and...love stories.

#1: Literature. Song lyrics you'll find in Psalms. You'll find poetry and riddles in Song of Solomon. Great fiction, too.

#2: Ah ha! I told you it was fiction.

#1: The only fiction you'll find in this book are actual made-up stories told by the best storyteller ever...a man named Jesus. And He told them to make a point in His teaching.

#3: *(to #2)* Let me see, will ya?

#2: Well...I guess...

#1: And before you ask, yes, there's love stories galore in that book.

#3: Let me see...

#1: Stories about parents loving their children. Husbands loving their wives. Friends loving their friends.

#3: *(raising a hand)* Me! Me!

#1: But the best love story in there can be found in the gospel chapters. Tells about God sacrificing His perfect Son for imperfect people like us.

#3: *(to #1)* Do you know if they have another copy?

#2: *(to #1)* How do you know so much about this book?

#3: *(to #1)* Yeah. You a librarian or something?

#1: No. I just know the Author of the book...and He knows me!

More

Words and Music by
SCOTT KRIPPAYNE, TONY MIRACLE
and CHARLIE PEACOCK
Arranged by Dennis Allen

With conviction ♩ = ca. 104

1. I used to read a - bout a man
2. When I think I've got You down,

who could walk a - cross the sea,
You move a dif - f'rent way,

*Two extra measures of drums on track.

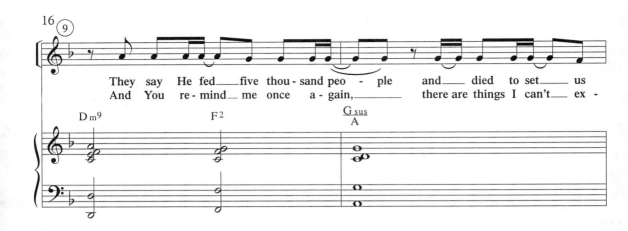

⑨

They say He fed five thou-sand peo - ple and died to set us
And You re-mind me once a - gain, there are things I can't ex -

Dm9   F2   Gsus/A

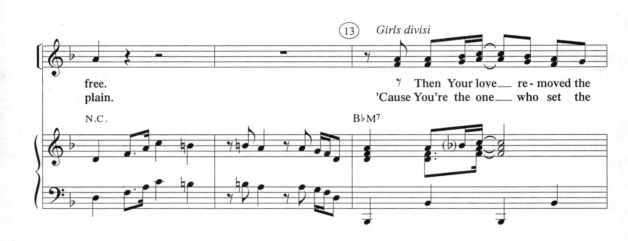

⑬ *Girls divisi*

free.
plain.

Then Your love re - moved the
'Cause You're the one who set the

N.C.   B♭M7

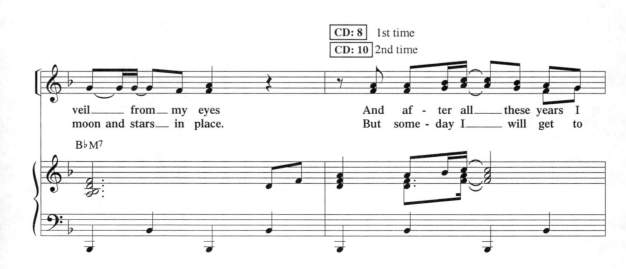

CD: 8 | 1st time
CD: 10 | 2nd time

veil from my eyes And af - ter all these years I
moon and stars in place. But some - day I will get to

B♭M7

18

The High Priest

Scripture Reading 1

from
Leviticus 9:7, Hebrews 7:27, 1 Peter 2:24

(music begins)

1: Moses said to Aaron the priest,

2: "Come to the altar, my brother, and offer your sin offering and your burnt offering, that you may make yourself right before God; then make the offering for the people, that you may make them right before God."

1: And God said to Jesus, the Promised One,

2: "Go, My Son, to the world and make of Yourself an offering for the people, that they may be right with Me."

1: Then Jesus, who knew no sin Himself, went to the earth and became sin on our behalf…

2: For He bore our sins in His body on the cross, that we might die to sin and live to righteousness: for by His wounds we are healed.

1: So now, we do not need a priest to offer sacrifices for us day after day. Jesus died once for us…

2: …and made us right with God…once and for all!

With a steady tempo ♩ = ca. 84

Music by DENNIS ALLEN

What's Done Is Done

NAN ALLEN

DENNIS ALLEN
Arranged by Dennis Allen

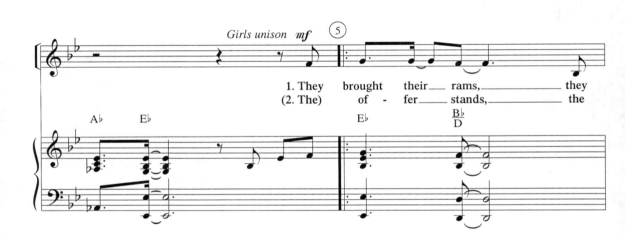

1. They brought their___ rams,_____ they
(2. The) of - fer___ stands,_____ the

brought their___ lambs,___ Laid them on the___ al - tar___ like
cov - e - nant.___ To de - ny it___ now,___ we cru - ci -

28

THE JOURNEY
Sketch

Characters:

> The Climber
>
> The Lord, an offstage voice
>
> The Swimmer
>
> The Runner

Props:

> long rope wound in a large circle
>
> swim goggles, swim fins
>
> track shoes

(Scene opens as The Climber enters with rope hung over shoulder, crossing to center)
(The Climber speaks as if to God.)

THE CLIMBER: Hey Lord. I'd climb the highest mountain for You. You know I would. I'm ready to climb, too. See, I've got new equipment. A good sturdy rope. The best that money can buy.

(entering from right, The Swimmer carrying goggles and swim fins, crossing to down right)

THE LORD: Nice. Very nice.

THE SWIMMER: *(speaking as if to God)*Yeah, and I'd swim the vastest ocean for You, Lord. I've been training. I even won the State Swim-off two years in a row!

(enter The Runner from left carrying track shoes or cross-country running shoes, crossing to down left)

THE LORD: Good. I'm proud of you.

THE RUNNER: *(speaking as if to God)* And Lord, I'd run the roughest track for You. Honest! I'm captain of my cross-country team, ya know.

THE LORD: Great. But will any of you walk with me through a dark, scary valley?

THE CLIMBER: *(unsure)* A dark...uh...scary valley?

THE LORD: Yes. And will you wait with me in the cold shadows of life?

THE SWIMMER: *(skeptical)* Hmm, how cold?

THE LORD: And will you stay with me in the deepest pit?

THE RUNNER: *(making an excuse)* Uh...I think I have a pit-phobia, Sir.

THE LORD: Oh. I see. *(beat)* Well...you know you won't grow as close to me at the highest point of a mountain...or racing through water at top speeds...or finishing the race in first place.

CLIMBER, SWIMMER, RUNNER: We won't?

THE LORD: I'm afraid not. You grow mostly in the valleys, in the shadows, and in the pit.

THE CLIMBER: Uh...are you gonna put us in all those places? The valleys, and shadows, and pits and stuff so we'll grow?

THE LORD: No, I don't do that. Those places just happen on their own.

THE SWIMMER: Well, do we have to go through those places?

THE LORD: Yes. Eventually everybody does.

THE RUNNER: But that's not fair. You're God!

THE CLIMBER: Yeah! You can wave Your hand and make everything all right!

THE SWIMMER: You're supposed to be good!

THE LORD: I am good. But life...well, sometimes life isn't. I just want to know that when the tough times come you'll stay with me.

THE CLIMBER: *(half-heartedly)* Okay. But what do I use all this rope for?

THE LORD: Maybe you can use it to anchor yourself when the storm comes.

THE SWIMMER: And what about all the training I did at the pool?

THE LORD: Use it to help you tread water when the floods arrive.

THE RUNNER: What about my new running shoes, Lord?

THE LORD: By all means...wear them to walk carefully when the road gets rough.

THE CLIMBER: Well...okay.

THE LORD: I'll be there, you know, every minute.

THE SWIMMER: All right.

THE LORD: I promise I'll never leave you.

THE RUNNER: I'm ready.

THE LORD: Good. *(beat) (as Climber, Swimmer and Runner are about to exit)* Oh,...and one more thing.

CLIMBER, SWIMMER, RUNNER: What?

THE LORD: You know...I'll even help you count your joys when it's all over.

(Climber, Swimmer, Runner look up and smile as lights fade)

The Well of My Soul

NAN ALLEN

DENNIS ALLEN
Arranged by Dennis Allen

36

40

Crucified with Christ

Words and Music by
RANDY PHILLIPS, DENISE PHILLIPS,
DON KOCH and DAVE CLARK
Arranged by Dennis Allen

48

The High Calling
Scripture Reading 2
from
1 Corinthians 9:24, Philippians 3:14, Philippians 4:8, Isaiah 40:31

(music begins)

#1: Do you not know that in a race all the runners run, but only one gets the prize?

#2: Run in such a way as to get the prize.

#1: Press on toward the goal to win the prize for which God has called (you) heavenward in Christ Jesus.

#2: Whatever is true…

#1: …whatever is noble…

#2: …whatever is right…

#1: …whatever is pure…

#2: …whatever is lovely…

#1: …whatever is admirable…

#2: if anything is excellent or praiseworthy – think about such things.

#1: Those who hope in the Lord will renew their strength.

#2: They will soar on wings like eagles…

#1: …they will run and not grow weary…

#2: …they will walk and not faint.

Music by DENNIS ALLEN

No Less

NAN ALLEN

DENNIS ALLEN
Arranged by Dennis Allen

1. Don't be mis-tak-en, don't be tak-en by the no-tion____ that
   cheap im-i-ta-tions, sub-sti-tu-tions that are claim-ing____ that

you can be-lieve____ on-ly what you can see.____
they can pro-vide____ more than God has to give.____

'Cause faith is as-sur - ance in what we hope___ and___
Quick - er an - swers, ne - go-tia - ble terms,___ ev - en

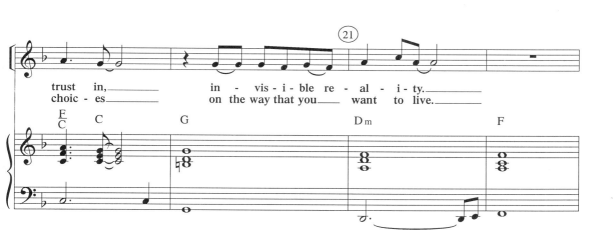

trust in,_____ in - vis-i-ble re - al - i - ty._____
choic - es___ on the way that you___ want to live._____

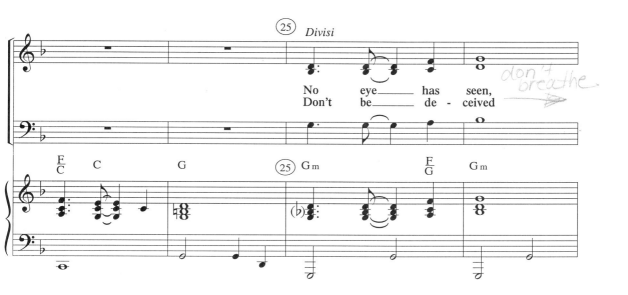

No eye___ has seen,
Don't be___ de - ceived

56

58

yours! The best, no less,___ is yours! The best, no less,___ is

yours! The best, no less,___ is yours!___

rit.

Testify to Love

Words and Music by
PAUL FIELD, HENK POOL,
RALPH VAN MANEN and ROBERT RIEKERK
Arranged by Dennis Allen

60

62

I will give thanks to God a - bove, For as long

as I shall live, I will tes - ti - fy to

CD: 47 1st time
CD: 48 2nd time
Divisi

104

Dm   Dm/C   Bb2(no 3rd)   Csus

1 (to pg. 67, meas. 92) Unison
love. For as long love.

2 Unison 109
With ev - ery breath I take

1 F2(no 3rd) (to pg. 67, meas. 92)
2 F2(no 3rd)
109
F2/A

I will give thanks to God a - bove,_____ For as long_____

Csus   C   Dm

113
Divisi

_____ as I_____ shall live, I will tes - ti - fy_____ to

113   Dm   Dm/C   Bb2(no 3rd)   Csus

116   staggered breathing

love.

116   F

Optional repeat and fade

The Water of Life

Scripture Reading 3

from
John 4:7-14

(music begins)

#1: There was a woman of Samaria who came to draw water. Jesus said to her,

#2: "Give me a drink."

#1: But the woman said to Him,

#2: "How is it that You, being a Jew, ask me for a drink since I am a Samaritan woman?"

#1: Jesus said,

#2: "If you only knew who you were talking to…you could ask and I would give you living water."

#1: And the woman asked,

#2: "Where do you find this living water?"

#1: Jesus answered,

#2: "Everyone who drinks of the water I will give him shall never thirst again; but within him will become a well of water springing up to eternal life."

Music by DENNIS ALLEN

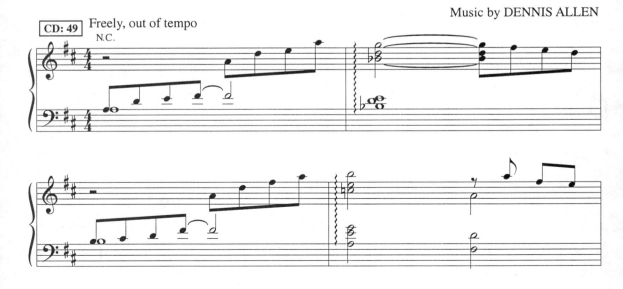

There Is a River

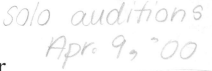

NAN ALLEN
Based on Psalm 46:4

DENNIS ALLEN
Arranged by Dennis Allen

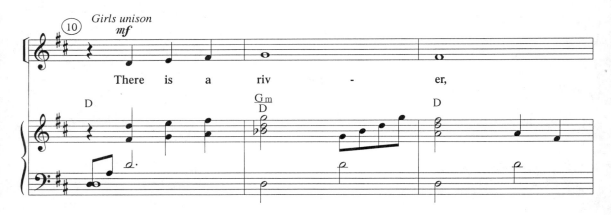

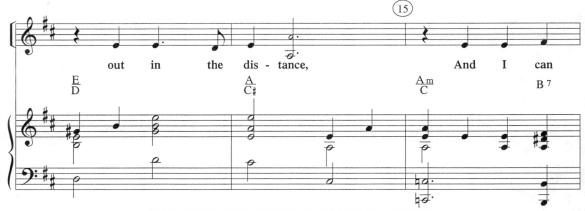

76

78

THE TRIAL

Sketch

Characters:

Jury, 10 to 12 people *(could be choir sitting on risers)*

Prosecutor

Judge

Accused

Defense Attorney

Bailiff

Classmate

Props:

chairs for Jury *(unless they sit on risers)*

tables, small (2)

chairs for Accused, Defense Attorney, Prosecutor, Classmate

table or high "bench"/chair for Judge

chair for witness

Bible

gavel

(Scene opens as "jury" is seated in two rows, the Prosecutor is standing behind a table at upstage right, the Accused and the Defense Attorney are seated behind a table at upstage left. The Judge is seated behind a table at down stage right. A witness chair is set at center. The Bailiff stands next to the witness chair.)

(Prosecutor is in the middle of his ((or her)) opening statements.)

PROSECUTOR: And so...your honor...and ladies and gentlemen of the jury, I submit to you that this person...the Accused...is guilty of the crime of withholding valuable, life-giving evidence from the Condemned.

JUDGE: Thank you, Mr. *(Ms.)* Prosecutor. So, Accused, how do you plead?

ACCUSED: *(starts to respond)* Your honor...I plead...

DEFENSE ATTORNEY: *(standing, interrupting)* The Accused pleads...not guilty.

ACCUSED: But...

JUDGE: I see. And so, Counsel, do you have witnesses to substantiate your client's plea?

DEFENSE ATTORNEY: I do, your honor. May I call my first witness...a classmate of the Accused.

(Classmate approaches the "stand")

BAILIFF: *(holding out Bible) (Classmate places left hand on the Bible and raises his right hand.)* Do you swear to tell the whole truth and nothing but the truth?

CLASSMATE: I do.

BAILIFF: You may be seated.

(Classmate sits in witness chair)

DEFENSE ATTORNEY: *(to classmate)* Now, would you please tell the court your relationship with the defendant.

CLASSMATE: Sure. Well, you see, we were classmates. Every year since sixth grade we were in the same homeroom. See, we were assigned alphabetically and his (her) name starts with "M" just like mine. *(starting to ramble)* Not that I liked my name, mind you. But what are you gonna do? I mean, your mother has a pet goat as a child with that name and then you come along...

JUDGE: *(banging gavel)* Just answer the question please.

CLASSMATE: Yes sir *(ma'am). (beat)* Uh, what was the question?

JUDGE: Your relationship with the defendant?

CLASSMATE: Oh, yeah. Classmate.

DEFENSE ATTORNEY: Good. Now did you at any time during your relationship with Accused ever feel he *(she)* was withholding important information?

CLASSMATE: Uh...no! I don't think. Well, there was this one time when I fell asleep in algebra class and I had this drool thing coming out of my mouth and he *(she)* didn't say a thing.

DEFENSE ATTORNEY: I'm talking about life-giving information here!

CLASSMATE: Oh. Well, the answer would be "no" then.

DEFENSE ATTORNEY: Thank you. Mr. Prosecutor, your witness.

PROSECUTOR: *(to Defense Attorney)* Thank you, Counsel! *(to Classmate)* Now, let me ask you to think back into your relationship with the Accused.

CLASSMATE: Okay.

PROSECUTOR: Was there ever a time when you were upset...or sad...or just confused about your life?

CLASSMATE: Sure. Who doesn't have those times?

PROSECUTOR: Can you recall one of those times?

CLASSMATE: Well, I remember one time when my grandmother died. I was pretty upset about that. When somebody dies like that...

PROSECUTOR: And did the Accused during that time talk to you about eternal life?

CLASSMATE: Well...not that I recall.

PROSECUTOR: What about when your best friend betrayed you and you felt like you couldn't trust anybody?

CLASSMATE: How did you know about that?

PROSECUTOR: Well, did the Accused share with you about a Savior who could be your best friend?

DEFENSE ATTORNEY: I object, Your Honor.

JUDGE: Overruled. Answer the question please.

CLASSMATE: Not that I recall.

PROSECUTOR: And did the Accused ever invite you to his *(her)* church?

CLASSMATE: Yes! Yes! He *(she)* did. Once...to help pick up trash after a big youth rally.

PROSECUTOR: A rally that you were invited to?

CLASSMATE: Well, no...I guess he *(she)* kinda thought that church and religious stuff was...personal...ya know.

PROSECUTOR: But it's not personal religious...stuff, as you say. The Accused possesses eternal life himself *(herself)*.

CLASSMATE: So?

PROSECUTOR: Would you like to know how you can live forever?

CLASSMATE: Sure! Doesn't everybody?

PROSECUTOR: No further questions, Your Honor.

DEFENSE ATTORNEY: *(standing slowly)* The defense rests.

(lights fade slowly)

You Don't Have the Right

Words and Music by
RANDY PHILLIPS, GERON DAVIS
and BECKY THURMAN
Arranged by Dennis Allen

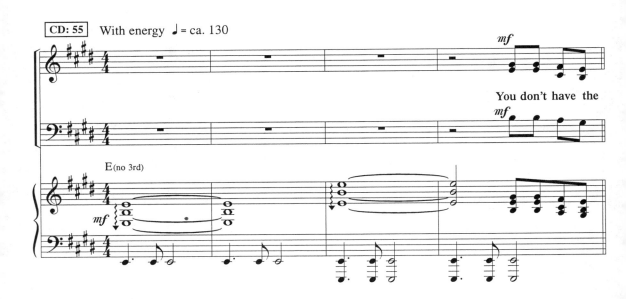

84

How Will They Know Us?

Scripture Reading 4

from
John 13:35, 1 John 4:11, John15:12,
Matthew 5:44, 1 John 4:7

(Music begins)

#1: God loved us and sent His Son.

#2: If God so loved us, we also ought to love one another.

#1: Jesus said, "This is My commandment, that you love one another as I have loved you."

#2: Love your enemies…

#1: …bless those who curse you…

#2: …do good to those who hate you…

#1: …and pray for those who spitefully use you and persecute you.

#2: Let us love one another, for love is of God.

#1: …and God is love.

#2: And Jesus said, "By this all will know that you are My disciples (that is) if you love one another."

Music by DENNIS ALLEN

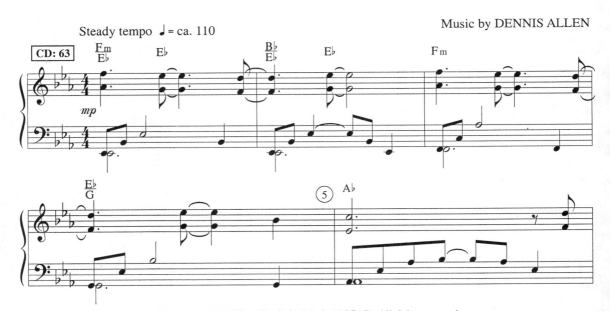

By This They Will Know

MARK ALLEN
and NAN ALLEN

MARK ALLEN
Arranged by Dennis Allen

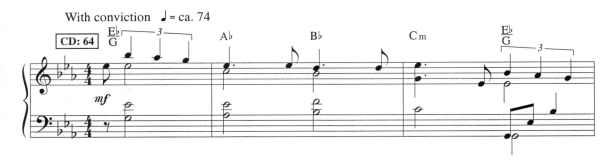

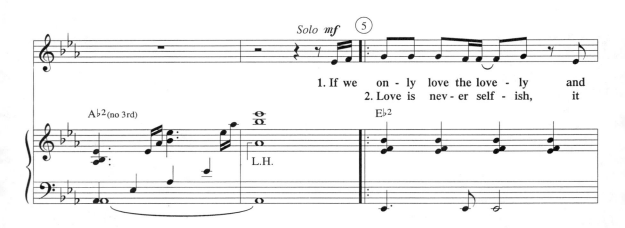

1. If we on - ly love the love - ly and
2. Love is nev - er self - ish, it

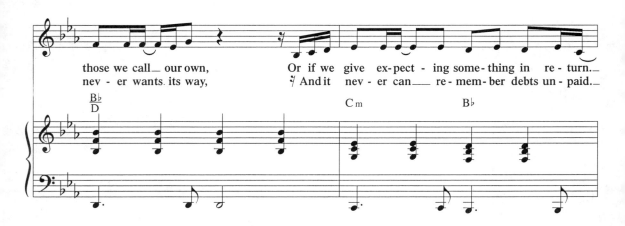

those we call__ our own, Or if we give ex - pect - ing some - thing in re - turn.__
nev - er wants its way, And it nev - er can__ re - mem - ber debts un - paid.__

Where is the proof___ that we be - long to___ Christ?___
There is the proof___ that we be - long to___ Christ.___

ah   We be - long to___ Christ.___ By this they will

Fm7   Ab/Eb   Bb/D   Eb   Eb/G

know   who Je - sus is.   By this they will   know   that we___ are

Ab   Bb   Eb   Eb/G   Ab   Bb

THE TREASURE
Sketch

Characters:

> Narrator, offstage voice
>
> Girl #1
>
> Guy #1
>
> Girl #2
>
> Guy #2

Props:

> three shoe boxes with lids
>
> piece of cloth, sized to fit one of the boxes
>
> ribbon, enough to wrap and tie around one of the boxes
>
> a draw string bag or a canvas bag
>
> small table, optional (for Girl #1 to put box on as she wraps it)

(Scene opens as Girl #1 enters with a small box, some cloth, and some ribbon)

NARRATOR: There once was a girl who bought a treasure so valuable that she wrapped it tightly in cloth to protect it.

GIRL #1: *(wrapping a small box with cloth)* There...that oughta do it.

NARRATOR: She tied it tightly with ribbons...

GIRL #1: *(tightly ties ribbon around the box)* That's good.

NARRATOR: ...and she held it tightly every minute of every day.

GIRL #1: *(holds the box very tightly with both arms)* You won't get away from me now. No sir.

(enter Guy #1 with a shoe box)

NARRATOR: Then there was this guy who bought a priceless treasure too, but he'd seen how uncomfortable the girl looked holding her treasure so tightly...

GUY #1: *(to Girl #1)* Yeah, get a life, will ya?

NARRATOR: So...he decided to carry his treasure loosely by his side.

GUY #1: *(takes the lid off the box and holds it loosely with one hand)* There...one hand free at all times...*(ala Big Bad Wolf)* the better to buy other treasures with, my dear.

NARRATOR: And there was a girl...

GIRL #1: What me again?

NARRATOR: There was another girl...

(enter Girl #2 with a shoe box in a draw string or canvas bag)

NARRATOR: She had a treasure, too. *(opens the bag and looks inside)* In fact, her treasure was an antique...handed down to her from many generations.

GIRL #2: None of that new cheap stuff for me.

NARRATOR: *(Girl #2 looks smugly at the others)* She had carried her treasure around all her life. She figured that with antiques, age is important.

GIRL #2: *(opens the bag again and looks inside)* How are you doing in there, ol' girl?

NARRATOR: Then there was this other guy who had a treasure.

(enter Guy #2, carrying nothing)

GUY #2: Hi, guys.

(others look suspiciously at Guy #2)

NARRATOR: He didn't buy his treasure at a store...or inherit it from an ancestor. He didn't carry it around in his arms or out to one side...or anything.

GIRL #1: I don't see anything.

NARRATOR: He kept his treasure inside his heart...

(Guy #2 smiles and looks toward heaven)

GUY #1: *(sarcastically)* Yeah, right!

(Guy #2 crosses to Girl #2 and mimes a conversation)

NARRATOR: And even more than that, he shared the treasure every day to everyone he met.

GIRL #2: *(to Guy #2)* I don't get it. How much did you pay for it?

GUY #2: It was free...actually.

GIRL #1, GUY #1, GIRL #2: Free?

(Guy #2 crosses to Girl #1, tries to talk to her)

GIRL #1: Must not be very valuable.

(Guy #2 crosses to Guy #1, tries to talk to him)

GUY #1: You get what you pay for.

GIRL #2: For real.

(Guy #2 crossing to down left, looking a little rejected)

NARRATOR: However, that guy's treasure did cost a lot. It had cost Someone His Son's life. But to our guy...it was free...and to anybody else who wanted it.

(Guy #2 crosses to others, trying one more time.)

GUY #2: Here. You guys want some?

GIRL #1, GUY #1, GIRL #2: No, uh thanks anyway, etc.

(Guy #2 crosses back to down left)

NARRATOR: Time came when all treasures had to be opened and displayed. *(Girl #1 begins to unwrap her box)* The first girl carefully unwrapped her treasure...peeling away first her tightly clasped arms...then the cloth and the ribbon...only to find that the rare treasure...was broken!

(Girl #1 opens lid of box)

GIRL #1: Oh, no! My treasure!!

NARRATOR: Though it had cost her a lot of money to buy, it was not guaranteed for eternity. And when she held it too closely...it broke into a million pieces. *(Girl #1 stands looking very sad)* Then it was the guy's...the first guy's turn to open his treasure.

(Guy #1 holds his box up)

GUY #1 Watch this everybody!

NARRATOR: But to his surprise. *(Guy #1 looks inside box)* His treasure was held too loosely.

GUY #1: *(looking all around)* What? Where is it? It was here just a moment ago.

NARRATOR: Maybe it was lost or stolen. Either way, it was gone...not guaranteed for eternity. *(Guy #1 stands looking very sad)* And then...the other girl, with her cherished antique carefully opened her treasure.

(Girl #2 takes box out of bag)

GIRL #2:   You'll all see what value really means.

NARRATOR: But apparently she had held her treasure too long, for when she exposed it to the elements...it rusted!

(Girl #2 opens lid of the box and looks inside)

GIRL #2:   Uh, oh. Anybody got any silver polish?

NARRATOR: Our last guy...the guy with the free treasure...hadn't worried about breaking, or losing his treasure...or having it damaged. His treasure was eternal.

(Guy #2 looks toward heaven with a smile)

GUY #2:   Eternal life, in fact.

NARRATOR: It was more valuable than any thing he could have bought or borrowed... or inherited.

GUY #1:   *(crossing to Guy #2)* And it was free?

NARRATOR: It was a free gift.

GIRL #2:   *(crossing to Guy #2)* I've been holding on to the wrong thing...for a long time. Guess it's too late for me.

NARRATOR: No. It's never too late.

GIRL #1:   *(crossing to Guy #2)* But I'm still holding nothing but a lot of broken pieces!

NARRATOR: Then let them go...

GUY #1:   But I've lost everything.

NARRATOR: Good. Then you're ready to hold onto something else...something that no matter how you hold it...will never let go of you.

Hold On to Jesus

Words and Music by
STEVEN CURTIS CHAPMAN
and JAMES ISAAC ELLIOT
Arranged by Dennis Allen

1. I have come to this o - cean
2. I've tried to hold man - y trea - sures.

and the waves of fear are start - ing to grow.
They just keep slip - ping through my fin - gers like sand.

The doubts and
But there's one

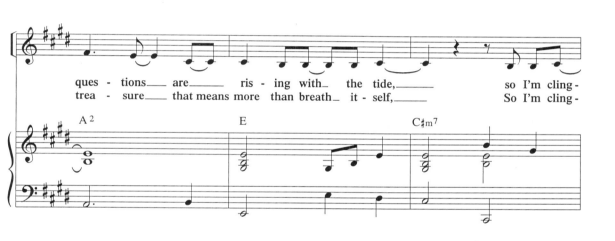

ques - tions___ are___ ris - ing with___ the tide,_____ so I'm cling-
trea - sure___ that means more than breath___ it - self,_____ So I'm cling-

CD: 70 1st time
CD: 72 2nd time

-ing___ to the one sure___ thing I___ know.
-ing to it with ev - ery - thing I___ am.

104

Commitment Medley

Change My Heart, O God
Trust in the Lord
Willing Heart

Arranged by Dennis Allen

*"Change My Heart, O God"

With feeling ♩ = ca. 100

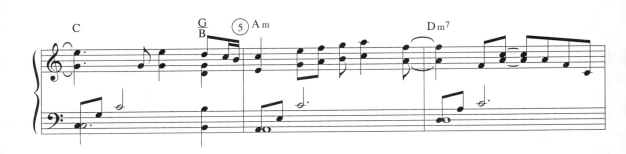

Pot - ter; I am the clay;

Mold me and make me, this is what I

CD: 79

(to pg. 110, meas. 9)

Girls unison

pray.

Trust in the Lord

*"Trust in the Lord"

116

*"Willing Heart"

*"Willing Heart"

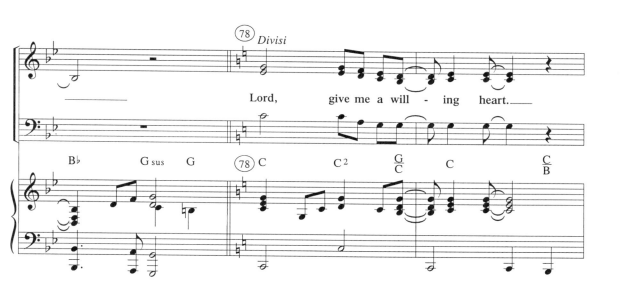

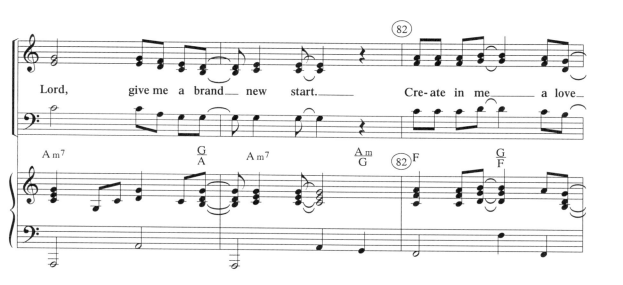

118

Worship Medley

Lifting Up My Voice
From the Rising of the Sun
Jesus, You Alone Are Worthy

Arranged by Dennis Allen

122

(to pg. 120, meas. 9)

wor - ship to You.

(to pg. 120, meas. 9)

*"From the Rising of the Sun"

Girls unison

A little faster ♩ = ca. 114

You. From the ris - ing of the sun

A little faster ♩ = ca. 114

to the go-ing down of the same, The

124

126

*"Jesus, You Alone Are Worthy"

Praise Medley

You're the Reason We Sing
Praise Him, Raise Him
Jesus Is the Rock

Arranged by Dennis Allen

*"You're the Reason We Sing"

130

Je - sus,___ we come___ to wor - ship___ Your name.___

You a-lone___ are wor - thy, we crown You King___ of kings.___

Ho - ly, ho - ly, ho - ly,

132

138

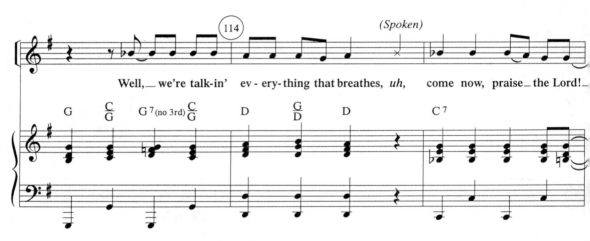

LIVE IT UP!

A Bible study
by Nan Allen

This collection of music and drama is designed to help you understand how you can "live it up"! As believers, we have rights, we have responsibilities, we have requirements, we have promises. The following Bible studies will help you discover what it means to live abundantly in your relationship with Jesus Christ.

I. ENJOY!

What is it like to win the state championship...to score the winning basket...to come in first in the big race? Talk about joy! You can't help but feel joyful in those circumstances.

But can you have the same joy even if you lose the game, foul out, or trip over your feet at the first turn? If you say yes, then where does that joy come from?

>Read Psalm 51:12. According to the psalmist, joy is a by-product of what?
>Read Galatians 5:22. According to Paul, joy is a what?
>Read James 1:17. According to James, joy, like all good gifts, comes from whom?

Now, whenever you sing the song "Living It Up", you can better understand what you're singing about!

II. DIG DEEPER!

Dig into the Word and find out more about the Father of lights mentioned in James 1:17.

Can you think about God in the three different roles in which He casts Himself–Father...Son...Spirit? It may be hard at first to think this way. But remember, you're one person, but you play different roles in life. Right? You're the child to a parent, a student to a teacher, a brother or sister to a sibling...and one day maybe a parent to a child. One person filling many roles.

>Each one of God's roles has many descriptions itself.
>For instance, God the Father can be referred to as Creator, Judge, Provider, etc.
>God the Holy Spirit is referred to as Holy Ghost and Comforter.

Now, what are some ways to describe God the Son? I'll give you a hint, then you think of some others.

Jesus		
Christ		
Messiah		
Savior		

Read Hebrews 3:1 and 7:26-28 from a paraphrase version of the Bible and from a modern translation. How is Jesus described in these passages?

Now, when you sing "More" and "What's Done Is Done" as you perform the sketch "Story Hour" and the reading "The High Priest," you'll be able to better communicate their messages.

III. ENDURE THE PAIN!

You've heard the phrase, "No pain...no gain". You've also seen T-shirts worn by believers that say, "His pain...your gain". Actually both of those statements are true. Read Hebrews 10:10. It tells us that without Christ's suffering on the cross, we could not have eternal life.

But, in Galatians 2:20 and in Galatians 6:14, God says we have to offer our lives, too. It says that we must be crucified with Christ

Now, does that mean that we literally must die physically to have a relationship with Christ? Why or why not?

Think about it. What kind of death was crucifixion? Was it cruel? Was it painful?

The scriptures mean that we must "put to death" the old life we lived before we came to Christ. We must "crucify" our old selves. Remember, crucifixion was painful. That means that the process of living like Christ won't be easy. We'll have to intentionally, painfully allow that part of our natures to die.

Make a list (mentally or on paper) of the things you know need to be "put to death" in your life. Is it anger? Is it lust? Is it bad language? Is it jealousy?

As you perform the sketch "The Journey" and as you sing "Well Of My Soul" and "Crucified With Christ", allow the Lord to help you put to death those things that hinder your relationship with Him.

IV. SLOW DOWN!

Don't you just love to wait in line? I'm kidding. I know you don't like to wait. Nobody does! Especially these days when everything is so...instant.

Think about it. Basically our world can give us what we want, when we want it! Information (internet), entertainment (cable TV), money (ATM's)...and so on! But all through scripture, God tells us we have to wait for Him if we want what He has for us.

Read Isaiah 40:31. This is a well known passage that tells us to wait. But with the command, there is a promise. What does God promise when we wait?
Lamentations 3:25 also promises something to those who wait. What is it?
Isaiah 26:3-4 doesn't use the word "wait", but it tells us we must "stay" and "trust forever" and when we do God will keep us in_____.
As you learn the song "No Less", and as you perform the reading "The High Calling," remember God's promises to those who wait for the best. And when you perform the reading "The Water of Life" and as you sing "There Is A River", think of sitting near a quiet stream and letting God fill you when you feel spiritually empty.

V. SPEAK UP!

The headlines read: CURE FOUND FOR ALL DEADLY DISEASES.

That would be some breakthrough! Imagine somebody developing a cure for cancer, for AIDS, for multiple sclerosis...every disease that kills people each day!

You have the cure! Not the cure for diseases of the body, but the disease of the soul... sin...the disease that causes eternal destruction.

Read Psalm 51:10-13. We usually read this passage of scripture as we ask God for renewal or cleansing of our lives. But read verse 13 again. The psalmist wants to be made right with God for what purpose?_____

We can communicate better today than ever before. As technology grows and infor-mation can be passed quicker and more efficiently than ever, why don't we seize the opportunity to tell the world that WE HAVE THE CURE! And His name is Jesus!

As you sing the songs "Testify To Love" and "You Don't Have the Right", and as you per-form the sketch "The Trial" realize the urgency to tell everybody you know about the cure for eternity spent in hell. We've got to keep telling the good news!!

VI. ACT IT OUT!

Hypocrite! That's a label nobody wants to wear. Right? How do you avoid it? Walk the Talk...as they say. In other words, if you sing about and talk about God's love for us, then you've got to love the other people God has created.

When Jesus was about to go to the cross, He gathered His twelve disciples in an upper room to give them last minute instructions.

Read John 13:34-35. What is Jesus trying to tell them? Basically, He was saying, "If you love me, you'll show it by loving other people...and not just those who are easy to love." He also said that love would be the way the world would know that they were His disciples.

In 1 Corinthians 13, sometimes called the "Love Chapter", Paul tells us how important love is to our message. Read verses one through three of the chapter. What things does he compare us to if we sing or speak about the Lord, but do not love each other? _____
_____

Perform the reading "How Will They Know Us?". Sing "By This They Will Know" and commit yourself to the love of others so that others can believe the gospel message you communicate.

VII. GIVE IT UP!

Read Romans 6:23 and Ephesians 2:8-9.

It's free. But it's not cheap. In fact, if anybody tries to tell you that eternal life (a relationship with God through Christ) won't cost you a thing, they're wrong. In fact, a salvation relationship will cost you everything.

Some people who actually met Jesus of Nazareth wanted to follow Him, but not enough to give up everything. One story in particular recorded in scripture is about a man called a rich young ruler. His story is found in Matthew 19:16-22. Read this and find out what the man was unwilling to give up for Jesus.

I said earlier that a saving faith will cost us everything. Then why was this man asked to give up only one thing? Could it be that Jesus knew that this one thing was the center of this man's life...the most important thing to him?

Another person Jesus required one thing of can be found in John 8:1-11. Who was the person and what did she have to give up? Hint: it is found in verse 11.
> Read Mark 2:14. Who was the person and what was he required to give up?
> Read about another man in John 3:1-4. Though it's not clear what this man was asked to give up, what do you think Jesus was sensing about the most important thing in this man's life?
> Philippians 3:7-12 is the price tag for a close relationship with the Lord.

Perform the sketch "The Treasure" and sing "Hold On To Jesus" as a commitment of everything you have to Christ.

LIVING UP

CONTEMPORARY SONGS AND SKETCHES FOR YOUTH

by Dennis and Nan Allen

LIVING IT UP

CONTEMPORARY SONGS AND SKETCHES FOR YOUTH

by Dennis and Nan Allen

LIVING IT UP

by Dennis and Nan Allen

CONTEMPORARY SONGS AND SKETCHES FOR YOUTH

LIVING IT UP

by Dennis and Nan Allen

CONTEMPORARY SONGS AND SKETCHES FOR YOUTH